Stone Fox

John Reynolds Gardiner

TEACHER GUIDE

NOTE:

The trade book edition of the novel used to prepare this guide is found in the Novel Units catalog and on the Novel Units website. Using other editions may have varied page references.

Please note: We have assigned Interest Levels based on our knowledge of the themes and ideas of the books included in the Novel Units sets, however, please assess the appropriateness of this novel or trade book for the age level and maturity of your students prior to reading with them. You know your students best!

ISBN 978-1-56137-063-4

Copyright infringement is a violation of Federal Law.

© 2020 by Novel Units, Inc., St. Louis, MO. All rights reserved. No part of this publication may be reproduced, translated, stored in a retrieval system, or transmitted in any way or by any means (electronic, mechanical, photocopying, recording, or otherwise) without prior written permission from Novel Units, Inc.

Reproduction of any part of this publication for an entire school or for a school system, by for-profit institutions and tutoring centers, or for commercial sale is strictly prohibited.

Novel Units is a registered trademark of Conn Education.

Printed in the United States of America.

To order, contact your local school supply store, or:

Toll-Free Fax: 877.716.7272
Phone: 888.650.4224
3901 Union Blvd., Suite 155
St. Louis, MO 63115

sales@novelunits.com
novelunits.com

Table of Contents

Summary 3

Introductory Activities 3

Ten Chapters 6
    Chapters contain: Vocabulary Words,
    Discussion Questions, Supplementary
    Activities, Predictions

Culminating Activities 18

Vocabulary Activities 21

Assessment for *Stone Fox* 23

Skills and Strategies

Thinking
Brainstorming, comparing and contrasting, evaluating, analyzing details

Literary Elements
Character, setting, plot development, story map

Vocabulary
Context clues, word mapping, classifying

Comprehension
Predicting, sequencing, cause/effect, inference

Writing
Narrative, descriptive

Summary	Faced with an extreme need for money to pay the taxes on their farm and to make Grandpa well, Little Willy enters the National Dogsled Race. Using his college savings for the entry fee, Willy is determined to win the race. But Stone Fox, an Indian and mountain man, is as intent on winning as Willy and he has a record of never losing a race.

Initiating Activity

1. Locate Wyoming on the U.S. map (setting for the story).

2. How are potatoes raised? Potatoes are important in this story. We all eat potatoes but probably most of you do not know much about where and how they are raised. Research topic.

3. Dog sled races are not common in all parts of the United States. In what states might we find dog sled races?

4. Not all pet dogs are good for dog sled racing. What kinds of dogs might be good? Research topic.

Instructions Prior to Reading:
Setting the Purpose

Previewing the Book	Have the students examine the cover. Ask: How old does the boy appear to be? What sort of expression does he have on his face? What is the background on the cover? *mountains* There is a man with more than one dog behind the boy. Who is he? Given the following clues from the cover, what do you think will happen in the story with--a boy and a dog--a sick grandfather--a race?
Recommended Procedure	This book will be read one section at a time using DRTA (Directed Reading Activity) Method. This technique involves reading a section, predicting what will happen next (making good guesses) based on what has already occurred in the story. The students continue to read and verify predictions at the end of each chapter.

© Novel Units, Inc.   All rights reserved

Using Predictions

We all make predictions as we read—little guesses about what will happen next, how a conflict will be resolved, which details will be important to the plot, which details will help fill in our sense of a character. Students should be encouraged to predict, to make sensible guesses as they read the novel.

As students work on their predictions, these discussion questions can be used to guide them: What are some of the ways to predict? What is the process of a sophisticated reader's thinking and predicting? What clues does an author give to help us make predictions? Why are some predictions more likely to be accurate than others?

Create a chart for recording predictions. This could be either an individual or class activity. As each subsequent chapter is discussed, students can review and correct their previous predictions about plot and characters as necessary.

- Use the facts and ideas the author gives.
- Use your own prior knowledge.
- Apply any new information (i.e., from class discussion) that may cause you to change your mind.

Predictions
_____
_____
_____
_____

Prediction Chart

What characters have we met so far?	What is the conflict in the story?	What are your predictions?	Why did you make those predictions?

Chapter 1
Grandfather
Pages 3-11

Vocabulary   explanation - p.4   harmonica - p.7   palomino - p.7
examination - p.9

1. Why did Little Willy think Grandfather's staying in bed was a new trick or joke? *p. 3-4 Grandfather had played lots of tricks.*

2. What is unusual about Doc Smith?
   --a woman
   --drives a horse
   --makes house calls
   --doesn't seem to have the usual doctor's office

3. When do you think this story takes place? There are time clues. What are the clues?
   --doctors making house calls
   --horse for transportation

4. Why do you think Little Willy lives with Grandfather? Does he have parents?

5. What do we know about Little Willy's dog?
   --name—Searchlight
   --ten years old
   --big black dog with a white spot on forehead

6. What do you think the problem is in the story?
   p.4   Grandfather will not get out of bed.
   p.9   Maybe a money problem.
   p.10 Doctor says Grandfather doesn't want to live any more.

Prediction   How will Little Willy find out why Grandfather doesn't want to live?

Story Maps

Many stories have the same parts--a setting, characters, a problem, a goal, and a series of events that lead to an ending or conclusion. These elements may be placed on a story map. Just as a road map leads a driver from one place to another, so, too, a story map leads a reader. There are many types of story maps. Students may use the one included on page 8 or make up their own.

It is suggested that the teacher make a large story map with the class as the story is read. This is displayed and as the characters are added or problems change, additions and corrections are made on the large map.

- Δ What information do we have to begin a story map?
- Δ Who is the main character?
- Δ What is the problem?

Story Map

Setting → **Problem** → **Goal** → **Episodes** → **Resolution**

Characters _____
_____

Time and Place _____
_____

Problem _____
_____
_____

Goal _____
_____
_____

Beginning ⟶ Development ⟶ Outcome
_____
_____
_____
_____
_____

Resolution _____
_____
_____
_____
_____

Using Character Webs

Attribute webs are simply a visual representation of a character from the novel. They provide a systematic way for students to organize and recap the information they have about a particular character. Attribute webs may be used after reading the novel to recapitulate information about a particular character, or completed gradually as information unfolds. They may be completed individually or as a group project.

One type of character attribute web uses these divisions:

- How a character acts and feels. (How does the character act? How do you think the character feels? How would you feel if this happened to you?)

- How a character looks. (Close your eyes and picture the character. Describe him/her to me.)

- Where a character lives. (Where and when does the character live?)

- How others feel about the character. (How does another specific character feel about our character?)

In group discussion about the characters described in student attribute webs, the teacher can ask for backup proof from the novel. Inferential thinking can be included in the discussion.

Attribute webs need not be confined to characters. They may also be used to organize information about a concept, object, or place.

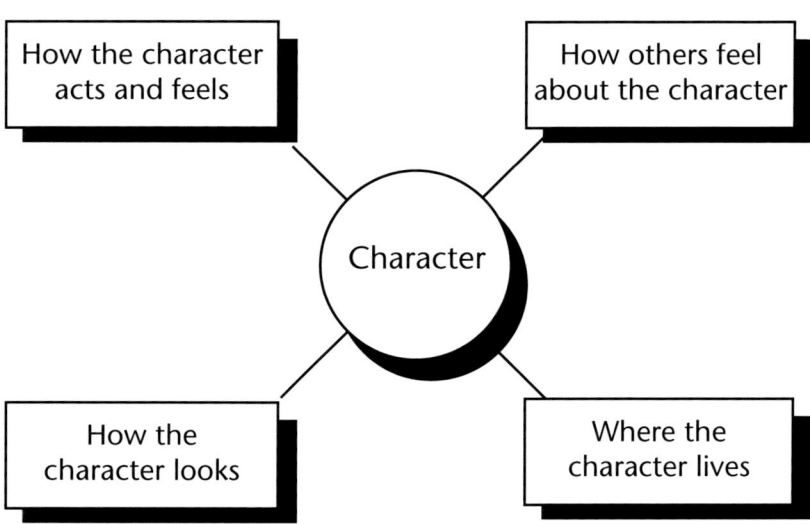

Activity Sheet
Attribute Web

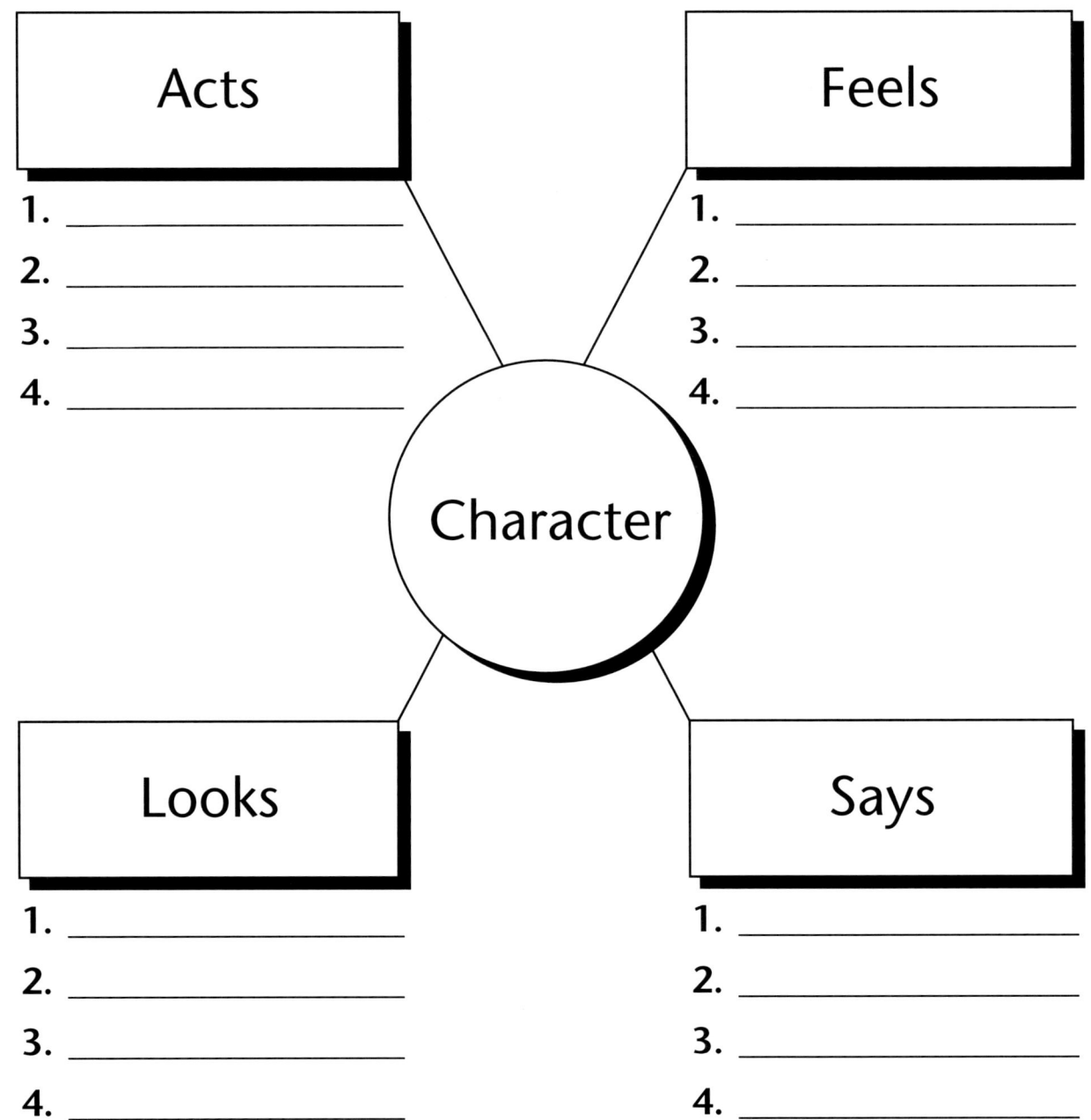

Chapter 2
Little Willy
Pages 12-21

Vocabulary   concerned - p.12   irrigation - p.12   harvest - p.13
inspected - p.16   mare - p.16   credit - p.17
mature - p.18   situation - p.18   determined - p.18

1. Let's begin an attribute web for Little Willy.

2. Doc Smith says Grandfather is going to die. What suggestions does she make? *p.13*
   --*put Grandfather in a nursing home*
   --*give Searchlight to a farmer*
   --*Little Willy could move in with the doctor until there are plans made*

3. How did Little Willy and Grandfather communicate?
   p.15-16 Sign Language

4. What steps were necessary for the harvest? *p.16*
   --*underground potato shed had to be cleaned*
   --*potato sacks had to be inspected and mended*
   --*plow had to be sharpened*
   --*horse for plowing had to be rented*

5. Do you think a ten year old boy could do this and go to school? Does Willy go to school? When do you think this story took place? Would that time make a difference? Why?

6. What did you learn about potatoes? Brainstorm Rules: all ideas count, add ideas

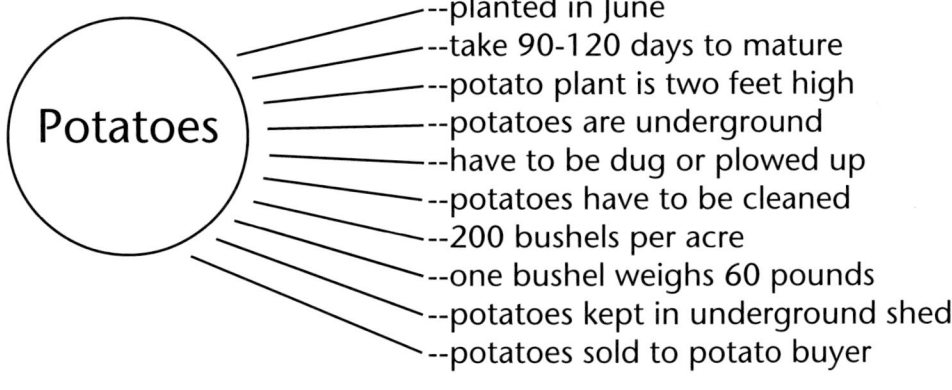

7. Do you think a dog could pull a potato plow? What kind of dog is Searchlight? *The author does not tell us. Research Working Dogs.*

8. Why hadn't Little Willy solved his problem when he got the money for the potatoes? *p.21 It wasn't the crop Grandfather was worried about.*

Prediction What is Grandfather's problem and how is Little Willy going to find out what it is?

Chapter 3
Searchlight
Pages 22-29

Vocabulary

stocked - p.23	outskirts - p.24	errands - p.24
deposited - p.26	respected - p.26	city slickers - p.26
blur - p.27	whereabouts - p.27	gully - p.27
enabled - p.27	tremendous - p.27	exhausted - p.29
impatiently - p.29		

1. How do you and your family get ready for winter? How did Little Willy get ready for winter?
   --chopped wood
   --stocked food

2. Why do you think Little Willy's school didn't start until October. *p.23 Boys and girls had to work on the farms until crops were harvested.*

3. How was Willy's life different from yours?
   Use a T-chart to show a comparison.

Willy	You
made breakfast	
fed Grandfather	
rides a sled to school	
runs errands after school	

4. What kind of fun did Little Willy have? *Racing his dog.*

Prediction Who was the impatient visitor on the porch?

Chapter 4
The Reason
Pages 30-36

Vocabulary
twang - p.30   ricocheting - p.30   derringer - p.30
authority - p.32   apparently - p.34   snatched - p.35
exposing - p.36

1. Chapter titles are important. What does this chapter title mean? Why did Grandfather not want to live?

2. Why did Clifford Snyder carry a gun? *p.32 Not a regular policeman; but taxmen have been threatened when they try to repossess a farm.*

3. Why do you think Grandfather didn't pay the taxes?
   p.34 There was not enough money.

4. Brainstorm the word **Taxes**.

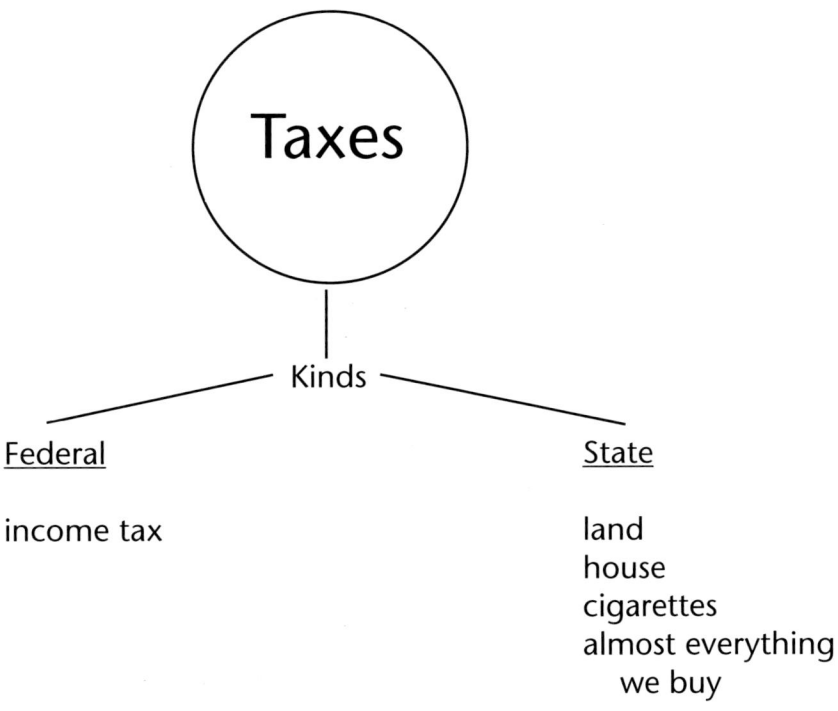

5. Mr. Snyder was not a pleasant man. Make a web for him. What are the best descriptive words for him?

Prediction How can Little Willy get five hundred dollars to save the farm and Grandfather's life? What would you do?

Chapter 5
The Way
Pages 37-45

Vocabulary   situation - p.37   bobbled - p.40   recommended - p.40
pried - p.43   saliva - p.43   Samoyeds - p.45

1. What does it mean to meet a situation head on? How would you say this?

2. Why do we pay taxes? *p.38 "Because it's the way the State get its money."*

3. What does the State and Federal Government do with the tax money? The teacher will use a T-chart and elicit student responses.

State	Federal
Roads	Defense-Army, Navy, Air Force
Schools	Washington D.C. Buildings
Health clinics	National Parks
Hospitals (some)	Salaries for:
	President
	Senators & Representatives
	Roads

4. Why does Little Willy live with Grandfather? *p.38 Little Willy's mother died.*

5. If you were in Willy's shoes, would you go to a bank president? How would you feel?

6. Why doesn't Willy sell the farm? *p.39 Willy believes if he pays the taxes, Grandfather will get better, but Grandfather will die if he sells or loses the farm.*

7. Why wouldn't the bank loan the money? *p.40 Because they didn't think Willy could pay it back.*

8. Why do you think Grandfather didn't use sign language to give his opinion? *p.42*

9. Find Jackson, Wyoming on the classroom map. Locate Utah on the map.

Research How fast can dogs run in dog sled races?
Are such races held today?

Prediction What kind of a chance do you think Searchlight and Little Willy will have in a race?

Chapter 6
Stone Fox
Pages 46-54

Vocabulary

funning - p.46	stunned - p.47	determined - p.47
amateurs - p.47	unison - p.50	granite - p.51
cunning - p.51	blurted - p.51	legends - p.51
awesome - p.51	contestants - p.54	

1. Why do you think the entrance fee was fifty dollars? *p.47*

2. Grandfather had said, "Where there's a will, there's a way." What does that mean?

3. What did you learn about Stone Fox? How did he look and act?

4. Why didn't Stone Fox talk to white men? *p.53 Because of the treatment the Shoshone Indians had received. They were forced to move from Utah to Wyoming.*

5. Why did Stone Fox race? *p.53 To make money to buy back the land that the white men had taken.*

Prediction Why didn't Stone Fox practice?

Chapter 7
The Meeting
Pages 55-61

Vocabulary   rooting - p.56   treacherous - p.57   departing - p.58
investigate - p.58   approached - p.60   motionless - p.61
massive - p.61

1. Why did Little Willy go to town at night? *p.56 To get medicine for Grandfather.*

2. How did Little Willy meet Stone Fox? *p.58 He investigated the sound of barking dogs in a deserted barn.*

3. Did he do anything to make Stone Fox angry? *p.58 He tried to touch Stone Fox's dogs.*

4. Why was it important that he talked to Stone Fox and told him why he had to win the race? *It showed Stone Fox what kind of boy Willy was.*

Prediction   Who will win the race?

Chapter 8
The Day
Pages 62-68

Vocabulary   swollen - p.62   abrupt - p.63   positioned - p.65
abreast - p.65   clenched p.67   tension - p.68

1. Did Willy tell people the truth about his black eye? Why not? *People would take it out on Stone Fox.*

2. Why didn't anyone bet on Willy and Searchlight? *He was just a boy. He belonged in the youngsters' race.*

3. Why do you think Willy has a chance at winning?

Chapter 9
The Race
Pages 69-76

Vocabulary   pursuit - p.70   disqualified - p.71   indicated - p.72
                   shrieked - p.73   glimpse - p.73   magnificent - p.73
                   effortlessly - p.74   steadily - p.74   regained - p.76

1. What advantage did Willy have over the other runners?
   p.70 "With only one dog and a small sled, he was able to take the sharp turns at full speed..."

2. Why do you think Stone Fox was in last place so long?
   p.71-73 To save his dogs for the big push at the end of the race.

3. Why was Little Willy distracted by seeing his Grandfather at the window? *p.72 Grandfather had been uninterested and unable to look out the window for some time.*

Chapter 10
Finish Line
Pages 77-81

Vocabulary   forged - p.77   challenger - p.78   approached - p.81

1. Were you surprised when Searchlight died? What other words describe how you felt?

2. Why do you think the author wrote this ending?

3. What kind of ending would you have written?

4. Why did Stone Fox draw a line in the snow and pull out his rifle? What was Stone Fox threatening? *p.81 "Anyone crosses this line--I shoot."*

5. Why did Willy carry Searchlight across the finish line?
   p.81 So he could be declared the winner.

6. Why do you think Stone Fox let Willy win?

Culminating Activities

1. Does this story have a hero? Is Willy a hero? Could Stone Fox be a hero? Divide the class into cooperative groups. The groups may decide if Willy or Stone Fox are heroes. Complete the Hero Attribute Web. See the Activity Sheet, page 19.

2. Write a chapter 11. What are all the happy things that could happen to Grandfather, Willy and Stone Fox? Will Willy get another dog? How will the townspeople treat Willy, the winner?

3. Write a paragraph describing how Little Willy changed in the novel. Give him a new nickname. Do pre-writing with a before and after the race or before and after Grandfather's illness.
Use a T-chart.

Willy before the Race	Willy after the Race

4. What was the author's message in this book? What is the most important thing to remember about this story?

5. Summarize the story using the story map. Which type of story map helps most? How would using a story map help you as an author? See the Activity Sheet, page 20.

Activity Sheet
Hero Attribute Web

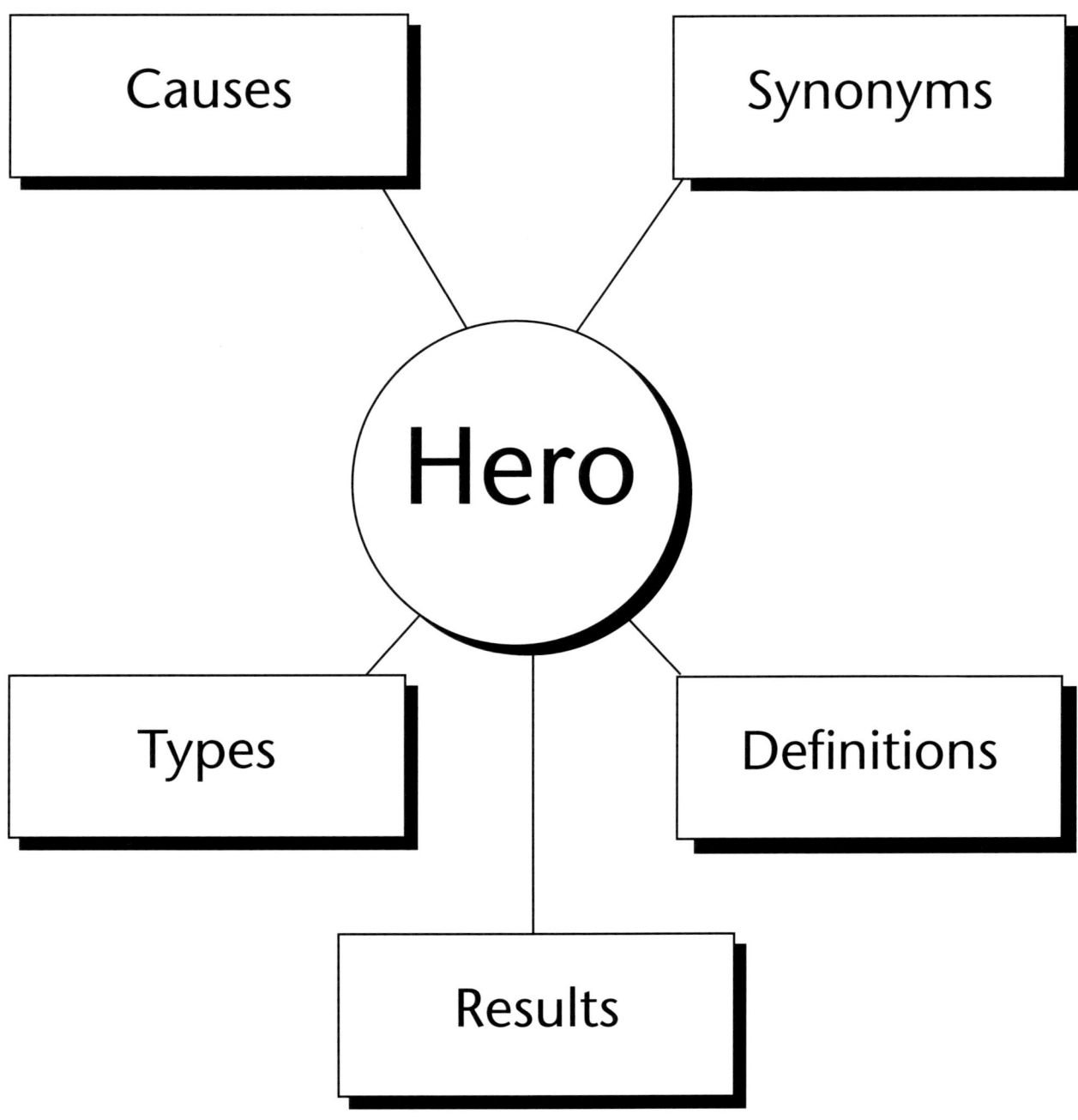

Activity Sheet
Story Map

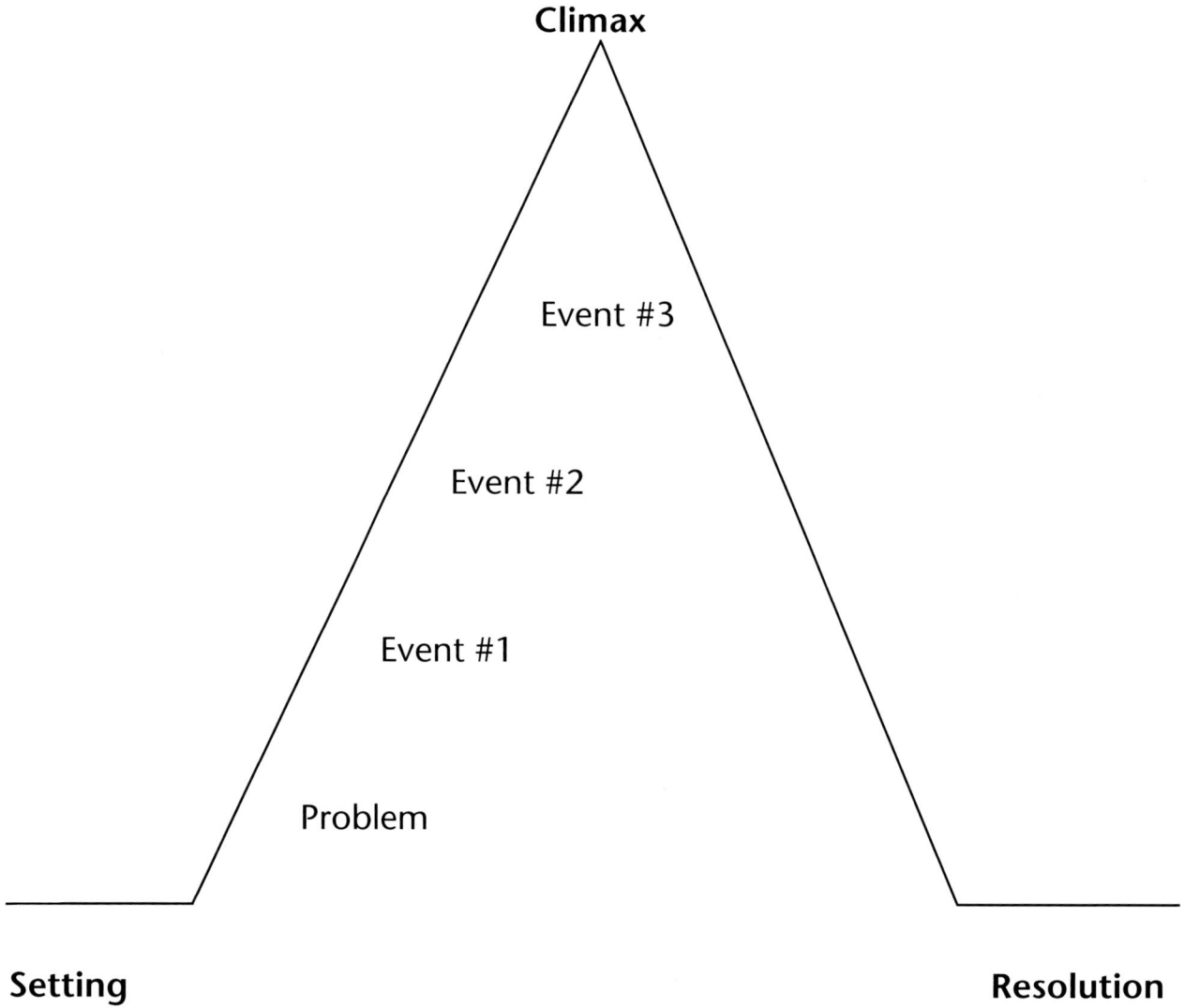

Vocabulary Activities

1. Develop word maps. Use color to distinguish antonyms, synonyms, etc.

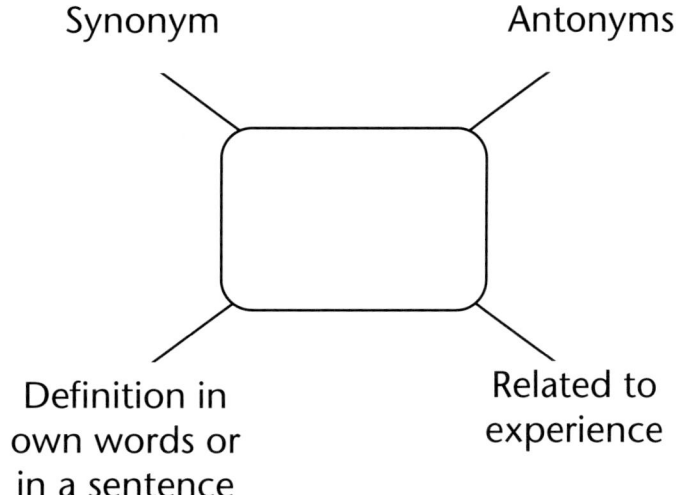

2. Crossword Puzzles--Have students use vocabulary words from the chapter to make crossword puzzles on graph paper. They should write a question for each word and develop an answer sheet. The teacher will check and then distribute the puzzles to other students to work out in their free time.

3. One student picks a word from the vocabulary list or cards. Another student has ten (or five) questions to discover the word and give the definition.

4. List vocabulary words on large sheets of paper. Leave space for students to a) illustrate the meaning next to each word; b) list a memory device to remember the word.

5. List the vocabulary words on the board or on a sheet of paper in the form of a table. Pronounce the words. Ask the students to rate their knowledge of each of the words (as a group, in cooperative groups or individually.)

Vocabulary Words	I Can Define	I Have Heard/Seen	I Don't Know

6. Provide vocabulary challenge words in context. Ask students to "guess" at the meaning from context, asking why for each guess. Generate a listing of the "why answers" to teach context clues.

7. Select ten words. Write only every other letter and a synonym or definition. Exchange student papers. Example: a_o_a: *(aroma)*.

8. Word Sort:
   I can say
   I know what it means
   I do not know

9. Word Sort:
   Action
   Things
   Places
   Names

10. I am thinking of a word that:
    has a long ā sound
    begins with the same sound as Pat
    means _____
    is a synonym of…

ASSESSMENT FOR *STONE FOX*

Assessment is an on-going process, more than a quiz at the end of the book. Points may be added to show the level of achievement. When an item is completed, the teacher and the student check it.

Name _____ Date _____

Student   **Teacher**

_____   _____   1. Write a journal for Willy as you read. Include ideas not found in the novel but which you think you can support.

_____   _____   2. Develop an attribute web for Willy as you read the novel. (See pages 9-10 of this guide.)

_____   _____   3. With a classmate, role play Willy talking to Stone Fox.

_____   _____   4. Divide a sheet of paper in four sections. What are the four most important parts of this story? Draw an illustration for each of these important parts.

_____   _____   5. Complete a research project on one of the following: dog sled racing, white men's treatment of Shoshone Indians, taxes.

_____   _____   6. Participate in discussion on Willy and Stone Fox as heroes.

_____   _____   7. Summarize the story using a story map. (See pages 8 and 20 of this guide.)

_____   _____   8. Complete at least six of the vocabulary activities.

_____   _____   9. Change three things in this novel and explain to a classmate how the changes would make a difference.

_____   _____   10. Write a chapter eleven. What are all the happy things that could happen to Grandfather, Willy, and Stone Fox? Will Willy get another dog? How will the townspeople treat Willy, the winner?

Notes